Lure
OF THE
Big Catch

H. NORMAN WRIGHT

Paintings by
SCOTT KENNEDY

HARVEST HOUSE PUBLISHERS
EUGENE, OREGON

"LORD HELP ME TO CATCH A FISH SO LARGE

that even I, in the telling of it, never need to lie."

EVREE ANGLA

Lure of the Big Catch
Text copyright © 2002 by H. Norman Wright
Artwork © 2008 by Scott Kennedy
Published in 2008 by Harvest House Publishers
Eugene, Oregon 97402
www.harvesthousepublishers.com

ISBN 13: 978-0-7369-1973-9
ISBN 10: 0-7369-1973-2

Design and production by Koechel Peterson & Associates, Minneapolis, MN

Artwork © 2007 by Scott Kennedy and used by Harvest House Publishers, Inc. under authorization.
For more information regarding Scott Kennedy's art or to obtain art prints,
     go to www.solsticearts.com.

Portions of this text are excerpted from *That's a Keeper* by H. Norman Wright (Bethany House Publishers, 2002).

Harvest House Publishers has made every effort to trace the ownership of all poems and quotes. In the event of a question arising from the use of a poem or quote, we regret any error made and will be pleased to make the necessary correction in future editions of this book.

Scripture references are from…

The HOLY BIBLE, NEW INTERNATIONAL VERSION®. NIV®. Copyright © 1973, 1978, 1984 by the International Bible Society. Used by permission of Zondervan. All rights reserved.

The New American Standard Bible®, © 1960, 1962, 1963, 1968, 1971, 1972, 1973, 1975, 1977, 1995 by The Lockman Foundation. Used by permission. (www.Lockman.org)

The Amplified Bible, Copyright © 1954, 1958, 1962, 1964, 1965, 1987 by The Lockman Foundation. All rights reserved. Used by permission. (www.Lockman.org)

The Living Bible, Copyright © 1971. Used by permission of Tyndale House Publishers, Inc., Wheaton, IL 60189 USA. All rights reserved.

Printed in Thailand

08 09 10 11 12 13 14 15 16 / IM / 10 9 8 7 6 5 4 3 2 1

CONTENTS

"*In the morning be first up,*

and in the evening last to go to bed,

for they that sleep catch no fish."

ENGLISH PROVERB

"THERE [THE FISHERMAN] STANDS,
DRAPED IN MORE EQUIPMENT THAN A TELEPHONE LINEMAN,
TRYING TO OUTWIT AN ORGANISM
WITH A BRAIN NO BIGGER THAN A BREADCRUMB,
AND GETTING LICKED IN THE PROCESS."

PAUL O'NEIL

HOOKING THE BIG ONE

You can have the smoothest, fastest, most creative setting technique, but if your hook isn't super sharp, forget it. You've got to have a hook that can penetrate every area of a bass's mouth. Some areas are hard gristle, and your hook may just slide over it and not dig in. Use quality hooks. Change hooks frequently. Sharpen your hooks…and keep them sharp.

JOHN WEISS

"It Takes More Than a Big Jerk," *The Best of Bassmaster*

A Keeper!

BEFORE THE ADVENT of the new fish mount techniques, great care was taken in wrapping and freezing a keeper so it would arrive at the taxidermist intact. Patiently we'd wait, often for several months, before that mount would be ready. And when it was, we'd let everyone know about it.

My first keeper mount wasn't really intentional. Have you ever made an off-the-cuff, thoughtless comment to your kids just to placate them and get them to mellow out? And then it backfires?

Before I discovered the joy of bass angling, trout was a mainstay. In the early '70s my family was fishing at Jenny Lake in Grand Teton National Park. Sheryl, my daughter, was 10 or 11 and constantly asking me when I was going to get a fish mounted. One morning as we walked through the forest to the inlet, she started in again. To settle this (and make sure I wouldn't have to fork out any money for a mount) I said, "Okay, when I catch a Yellowstone cutthroat over 20 inches, I'll do it." She was satisfied, and I was smug…until an hour later when I held up a brilliantly colored, twenty-one-inch cutthroat. Sheryl was ecstatic. I have to admit I was excited too, but obviously I was going to be a bit poorer. It was worth the cost though. What a keeper!

Sheryl caught a keeper 20 years later. We took pictures, weighed and measured, and released it back into the water. The "mount" of this 22-pound northern pike ended up on the wall of her nail salon. Since she owned the place, she could decorate any way she wanted. You should have heard the reaction of some of those prim and proper, fastidious clients! And by the way, can you guess who paid for this mount? It never ends when you have a daughter.

"It's a keeper!" isn't limited to fishing. You and I are "keepers." In fact, every person ever created is a keeper in God's eyes. There's no culling that occurs on His part. No matter our size, shape, age, gender, color…it's all the same to Him. He created us and loves us. "God so loved the world that he gave his one and only Son, that whoever believes in him shall not perish but have eternal life."

It's Dangerous Out There

EVERY FISHING LOCALE has its own built-in dangers. They come in many forms: unexpected weather changes, a sunken snag that rips a hole in the bottom of your boat, animal problems. Yes, animals. Have you ever had bees drive you away from a prime fishing spot? It can happen, and it did happen. My nephew and I were walking the Jocco River in Montana. As we worked our way along the bank, we saw a couple of likely spots just ahead. We pushed through the bushes and cast out, not realizing the spot was already taken…by a number of unhappy, grudge-carrying bees. We didn't argue. Sorry, but fish aren't worth bee stings, especially when I'm allergic to them.

What about bears? We went downstream a mile, rounded a bend, and found a great spot. Across from us was a large patch of wild berry bushes. It seemed strange that a number of these thorny bushes were shaking when there was no wind. All of a sudden a big black head popped out of the bushes about thirty-five feet away and looked right at us. Then a second head emerged with the same stare. A third popped out and gave a grunt. It was the proverbial three bears, but this time it was a mom and her nearly grown cubs. We thought, *This is our fishing hole—beat it, bears!* The bears thought, *This is our berry patch; the river isn't that wide or deep, so get lost, people!* We did. Being watched and evaluated as a possible meal somehow takes the fun out of fishing.

What about fleas? That's right—fleas! My wife, Joyce, and I were fishing off a sandy beach on Yellowstone Lake on our anniversary a number of years ago. The fish were going wild. The sun got hotter, and I took off my shirt, laid it on the sand, and kept casting. When we finished, I put the shirt back on, and we drove back to our cabin in Grand Teton National Park. When I took the shirt off to take a shower, I was shocked. My upper body was covered with scores of bites—flea bites. The fleas in the sand hitchhiked on the shirt to get a free ride and free meal. We spent a few hours dabbing calamine lotion all over my body. I can think of better ways to spend an anniversary afternoon!

And then there are snakes. A snake can ruin the best day of fishing. An angler out on Lake Irvine stopped his boat one morning and stood on one of the seats in the back. That's not too unusual. I've seen a number do this off the shoreline as they cast for bass. But he was in the middle of the lake, had no rod in hand, and was yelling his head off. It seemed a rattler had crawled into the boat the night before, and when the sun came out and warmed his body, he came alive. So did the boatman. Fortunately someone came along and bailed out the snake.

I was fishing for largemouth bass with a guide at Euchi Lake in Oklahoma in the early springtime. Foliage was just starting to fill in the thick forest and heavy undergrowth around the lake. The guide's instructions were interesting: "If you cast a plastic or even an expensive lure or spinnerbait on the shore and hang it up, just break it off. We don't retrieve them." That seemed strange and a bit expensive, especially when the lures were in plain sight. He went on to describe an experience with a client who struck a log on shore with a 10- to 15-dollar lure. He wanted to retrieve it in the worst way. The guide said, "Well, we can do that if you're set on gettin' it back, but what're you goin' to do with that cottonmouth sittin' next to it?"

Our guide went on to say that the shoreline was so infested with snakes that he never got out of the boat.

That's good advice. Sometimes we need to protect ourselves, so we make preparations by checking out the terrain, asking advice of locals, keeping our eyes open, and carrying something in case we're attacked—like pepper spray.

My friend bought some, and as we exited his car in his garage, he pulled it out and read the instructions. But he went a step further. He decided to test it…in the garage. He walked away from the car, sprayed it, and walked back. A couple of minutes later he walked across the garage right through the spray that was hanging in the air. After he quit coughing, sneezing, and having his eyes water, Gary said, "Man, that stuff works." As I opened my mouth to make a kind remark, I breathed some of it in—and got out of there fast. Don't test it inside! It's worse than some of those critters out there.

Sometimes you need to protect yourself against other things in life as well. People can give you bad advice. People can tempt you. Satan can tempt you. Just as you stay away from bees, fleas, bears, and snakes, keep yourself from everyday dangers. God's Word says to get away from temptations: "Flee the evil desires of youth, and pursue righteousness, faith, love and peace." What do you need to run from?

"Even if you've been fishing for three hours
and haven't gotten anything except
poison ivy and sunburn,
you're still better off than the worm."

AUTHOR UNKNOWN

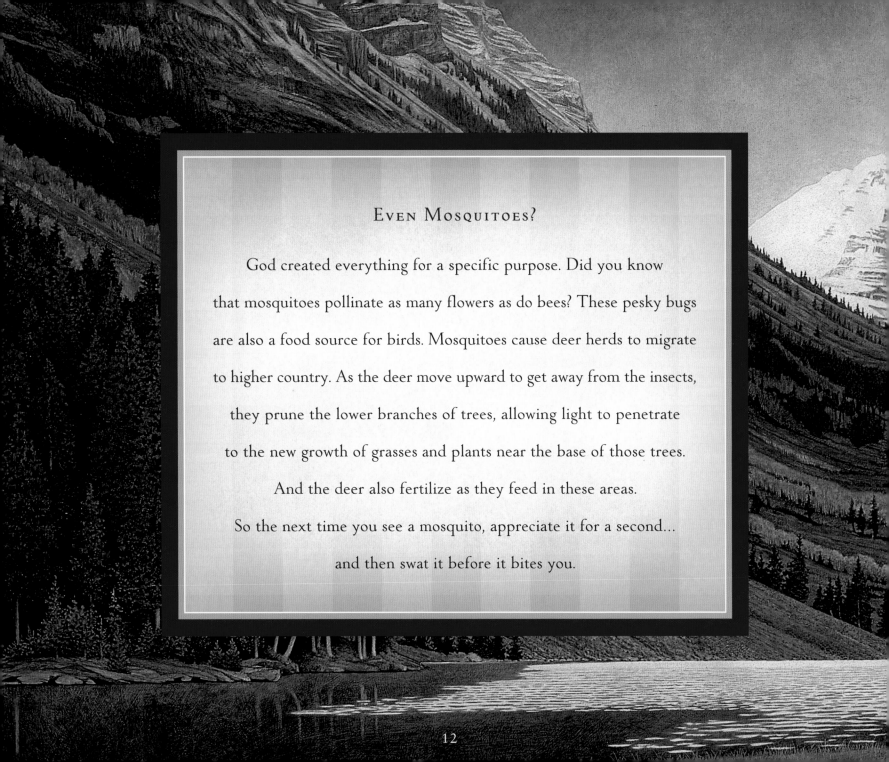

Even Mosquitoes?

God created everything for a specific purpose. Did you know

that mosquitoes pollinate as many flowers as do bees? These pesky bugs

are also a food source for birds. Mosquitoes cause deer herds to migrate

to higher country. As the deer move upward to get away from the insects,

they prune the lower branches of trees, allowing light to penetrate

to the new growth of grasses and plants near the base of those trees.

And the deer also fertilize as they feed in these areas.

So the next time you see a mosquito, appreciate it for a second...

and then swat it before it bites you.

"Fishing is much more than fish.
It is the great occasion when we may
return to the fine simplicity
of our forefathers."

Herbert Hoover

Heeding Advice

A FRIEND AND I WERE at one of the largest fishing and boating shows in California. As we strolled the aisles we noticed one of the exhibits for salmon fishing in Alaska. It was like many others, except the guides manning the booth were all women. As we talked with them, I asked if many women went on their excursions. They told us quite a few did, and then they added a comment I didn't expect: "And they always catch more fish than the men."

"Why is that?" I asked.

"It's simple. The women listen to what we tell them to do. They're more open to instruction than the men." Interesting. That's quite a commentary on men. That is, if that's *really* true. (How's that for a typical male response?) But, admittedly, I've heard the same comment from other guides, including men. A couple of bass guides complained to me about the very same thing. One said, "I wonder why some clients bother to hire me for a day. They end up telling *me* how they're going to catch fish with their dumb lures. It usually takes a couple of hours for them to listen." (As for me, when I'm out with a guide who's been bass fishing for years, I want every bit of knowledge he's got.)

What is it about males that makes them resistant to instruction and advice? Some men seem to have a need to show how much they know about something. Fishing isn't the only place men aren't that open to instruction. They often react the same way in marriage relationships (yeah, yeah, I know I'm meddling now). I remember reading the following about men (and I remember my reaction). Here's the gist of what was said:

- Men hate to be wrong. (I'm not sure I agree with this.)
- They hate being told they're wrong. (True.)
- They hate even to suspect that they might have been wrong. (Whoa! That's going a bit too far.)
- And most of all, men hate it when a woman knows they are wrong before they know it themselves. (Very true.)

- The tricky part is that men feel they are being "made wrong" or told they did something wrong, when women aren't telling them that at all. (Guilty as charged.)

I found an interesting study about "marriages that last" compared to those that don't. After all was said and done, it came down to one principle: "Newlywed men who listened to what their wives said and did it ended up with stable marriages."[1] And I'm sure it works the other way too.

There's another source for telling everyone to listen to advice. It's God's Word. Consider these words the next time you're tempted to tune out that person giving you advice:

- Be not wise in your own eyes.
- A man who refuses to admit his mistakes can never be successful. But if he confesses and forsakes them, he gets another chance.
- He who leans on, trusts in, and is confident of his own mind and heart is a (self-confident) fool, but he who walks with skillful and godly wisdom shall be delivered.

If you want some real advice that can change your life, read the book of Proverbs and then apply it. Your work relationships, your family relationships, and your fishing relationships will all see a difference.

"All you need to be a fisherman is patience and a worm."

HERB SHRINER

"The two best times
to fish is when
it's rainin' and when it ain't."

PATRICK F. McMANUS

> "I'M A BIG HUNTER AND FISHERMAN. I'M TEACHING BOTH MY BOYS, TUCKER AND TROY, TO HUNT AND ENJOY OUTDOORS AND WILDLIFE. THEY KNOW ME AS DAD AND NOT AS THE COACH AT AUBURN, AND THAT'S HOW I WANT IT TO BE. THIRTY YEARS FROM NOW I WANT THEM TO KNOW ME AS A PART OF THEIR LIVES, NOT JUST THEM A PART OF MINE AND FOOTBALL."
>
> TOMMY TUBERVILLE

People Are Not Bass

YOU'RE 15 FEET UNDER the surface of the lake. Above, the sun is shining, the trees on the shore are various shades of green and brown, and the sky seems endless. It's a different story where you are. It's murky and what vegetation there is seems drab and lifeless. A crawdad skirts from the protection of one rock to another, and a couple of shad slip by. There are two or three large boulders and an aged tree stump, and that's all. But hold it. There is something else.

There's a large, solitary shape between the tree and one of the rocks. You look closer. It's a bass—a *large* bass with a torn fin and a few scars on its body. There are no other fish around. And that's the way she wants it. She's alone and in a world of her own. When she sees a school of shad she doesn't alert any other bass so they can share in the feast. Nor does she work together with three or four others to ambush and harvest the shad. Her motto is, "I'd rather do it myself," and she does. No hassles with other bass. No responsibility. No accountability. She lives life by herself, for herself, with no interaction with other fish.

"I STILL DON'T KNOW WHY I FISH OR WHY OTHER MEN FISH, EXCEPT WE LIKE IT AND IT MAKES US THINK AND FEEL."

RODERICK L. HAIG-BROWN

Even when you see a school of bass, they're hanging out together but they're really *not* together. They have no interaction, no accountability, and no fellowship.

But people are created for relationships. And relationships include accountability. We're not to be islands or solitary "trophy bass." Relationships are one of the most significant elements of human life. Most of our lives are spent in various relationships. Take them away and our existence becomes sterile. Sure, there are those who appear not to need them, but they're the exceptions.

Max Lucado has something to say about relationships:

A RELATIONSHIP. THE DELICATE FUSION OF TWO HUMAN BEINGS. THE INTRICATE WEAVING OF TWO LIVES; TWO SETS OF MOODS, MENTALITIES, AND TEMPERAMENTS. TWO INTERMINGLING HEARTS, BOTH SEEKING SOLACE AND SECURITY.

A RELATIONSHIP. IT HAS MORE POWER THAN ANY NUCLEAR BOMB AND MORE POTENTIAL THAN ANY PROMISING SEED. NOTHING WILL DRIVE A MAN TO GREATER COURAGE THAN A RELATIONSHIP. NOTHING WILL FIRE THE HEART OF A PATRIOT OR PURGE THE CYNICISM OF A REBEL LIKE A RELATIONSHIP.

WHAT MATTERS MOST IN LIFE IS NOT WHAT LADDERS WE CLIMB OR WHAT OWNINGS WE ACCUMULATE. WHAT MATTERS MOST IS A RELATIONSHIP.[2]

How would you describe your relationships with others? How would they describe them?

And then there's accountability. To whom are you accountable? Who is accountable to you? Why be accountable? Patrick Morley describes it for us:

> THE PURPOSE OF ACCOUNTABILITY IS NOTHING LESS THAN TO EACH DAY BECOME MORE CHRIST-LIKE IN ALL OUR WAYS AND EVER MORE INTIMATE WITH HIM.
>
> UNLESS WE ARE ANSWERABLE ON A REGULAR BASIS FOR THE KEY AREAS OF OUR PERSONAL LIVES WE, LIKE SHEEP, WILL GO ASTRAY. YET, TO SUBMIT OUR LIVES FOR INSPECTION TO SOMEONE ELSE GRATES ON OUR DESIRE TO BE INDEPENDENT. WHILE WE DESIRE TO LIVE LIKE A CHRISTIAN, WE OFTEN WANT TO KEEP IT JUST BETWEEN "ME AND JESUS." BUT THE WAY OF THE SCRIPTURES POINTS TO ACCOUNTABILITY AMONG BELIEVERS.[3]

Here are some great biblical words of wisdom that will enhance your relationships!

- Carry each other's burdens.
- Look to the interests of others.
- Love one another.
- Two are better than one. If one falls down, his friend can help him up.

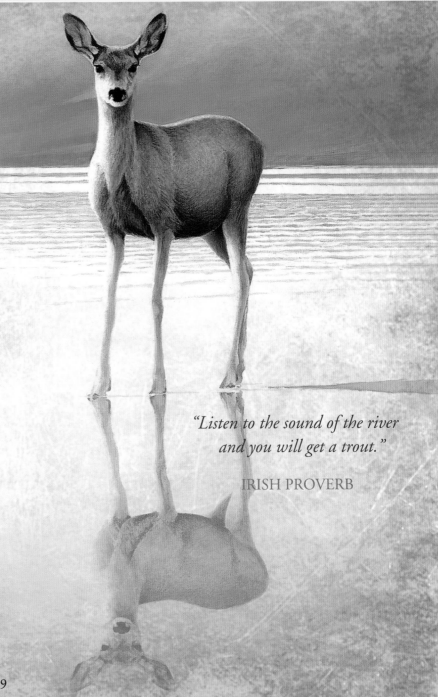

"Listen to the sound of the river and you will get a trout."

IRISH PROVERB

> "DO NOT TELL FISH STORIES WHERE THE PEOPLE KNOW YOU;
> BUT PARTICULARLY, DON'T TELL THEM
> WHERE THEY KNOW THE FISH."
>
> MARK TWAIN

It Weighed How Much?

YOU COULD HEAR the two anglers from several hundred yards away. Every time they boated a bass, one would say, "Look at the size of that fish! This is great."

As I cruised by I asked how it was going. They said, "Man, we've hit a school of good ones. Every fish has been over three pounds." And they held up their latest catch for me to see before they released it. The problem was, it didn't look like any three-pounder I'd ever seen (and I tend to be a stickler for accuracy, especially when it comes to fish).

I stopped a good distance away and immediately tied into a bass. Once it was boated, one of them yelled over, "I see you found that school too."

I said, "Looks like it." They watched as I took out my digital scales to weigh it. I was curious as to what it really weighed. Right at a pound and a half. I was sort of hoping they wouldn't ask what it weighed, but they did. When I told them, they were good sports and said, "I guess we were off a bit. Oh well, we'll just revise our guesstimate downward. At least they're still a lot of fun." And that they were.

Weight used to be important. But weight can vary depending on the scale, since very few scales are certified. Today there's more emphasis on length. An inch is an inch. A problem arises when you try to use length to determine weight. A 21-inch bass can weigh 5, 6, or even 7 pounds. Some fish look as though they've been to Weight Watchers, while others are virtual food machines in appearance. I fish one lake where most of the bass look underfed and undernourished, and another where they resemble footballs. And as you would guess, the bigger the bass, the more weight it gains for each inch it grows.

Studies show a considerable variation of weight even at a given length. For example, the average 22-inch bass from Florida weighs about 6½ pounds, which is similar to the standard weight. But surveys conducted by biologists found bass that length that weighed as little as 4½ pounds to as heavy as 8 pounds. That's quite a variation.

You're probably aware of the conversion method that most anglers use:

$$\frac{(girth \times girth) \times length}{800} = weight$$

This works for some fish, but not very well with those that are almost as round as they are long. Biologists in California have developed a formula that seems to work better on bass that are longer than 22 inches with a girth over 21 inches:

$$\frac{(length \times length) \times girth}{1000} = weight$$

Even so, it's still not 100 percent accurate. Perhaps you've heard about bass fisherman Bob Crupi of California. (Bob also guides, and I've gone on several trips with him. Not only did I catch huge bass but I also learned much from his years of experience.) He's the only one who's landed two bass over 20 pounds. He weighed his 1991 fish on a certified scale and it came out 22.01 pounds. Using the new formula, however, it would have come in at 23.9. That would have been a world record. Unfortunately, it wasn't.

You may want to use these formulas to get a general idea. That's better than eyeballing your bass and then (unconsciously, of course) throwing on a couple of pounds for good measure. But the best way is to get a good digital scale (and get it certified).[4]

> "FISH COME AND GO,
> BUT IT IS THE MEMORY OF AFTERNOONS
> ON THE STREAM THAT ENDURE."
>
> E. DONNALL THOMAS

Where Eagles Fly

HEY, I'M TOO BUSY TO GO FISHING." Not too many true anglers make that statement. But "busy disease" is always lurking around the corner waiting to infect our lives. And when it does, say goodbye to the presence of joy. The two are not compatible.

I've been on lakes where the scenery and wildlife are like a *National Geographic* documentary. Even if the fishing wasn't good, the surroundings made up for it. I've made comments to other anglers about rugged cliffs, the lush vegetation, or various wildlife. Sometimes I hear in response, "I didn't notice. I'm too busy trying to find some bass."

Well, it's true that fisherman can be single-minded and incredibly focused, but all it takes is a minute to stop, look around, and listen. Sometimes sound calls you back to what you're missing. It could be the gentle breeze rustling the leaves of the trees, the cry of a hawk, the call of a loon, or the splash of a beaver. Look up; look around. What you see may be on par to or better than catching a large bass or trout or walleye.

One day when I was shore fishing on a small mountain lake, I heard a noise and looked up. Two bald eagles were fighting with a golden eagle over a fish one of them had caught. They tumbled through the air again and again. I stopped fishing to watch a sight I'd never seen before and perhaps will never again.

Busyness can keep us from getting the most out of life. Even bass pros battle this problem. Some folks say they wish they could have the life of a pro—all fishing pros have to do is fish and get paid for it. Obviously they've never talked to a pro in detail. One told me he was away from his home for four months straight. He'd finish a tournament, go on to a sports show to promote a boat or rod for one of his sponsors, drive to another lake to pre-fish for three days, fish the tournament, and then drive to the next show. In the meantime he had to keep up his boat, change his fishing line, replace lost lures and other items, and keep in contact with his family. You get the picture. Some may thrive on this; others get worn out. This guide said his lifestyle cost him his marriage. Yes, he was too busy.

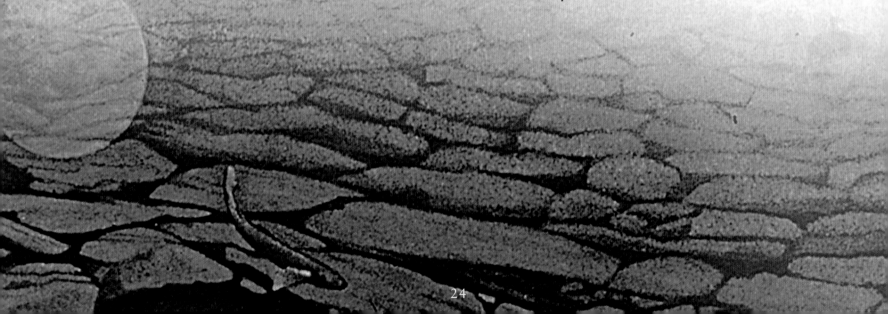

It's too bad life gets so harried, but most times it's our choice. We choose to add to our schedules or we refuse to cut something out. Being too busy impacts our life in many negative ways. It can cloud our judgment and discernment. When we have too much to do we don't take the time to think through decisions. Mahatma Gandhi said, "There is more to life than increasing its speed." Someone else said, "Nothing done impulsively and in a hurry is ever well done…We always do fast enough when we do well. Drones make more noise and are more in a hurry than the [worker] bees, but they make no honey. Thus those who rush around with tormenting anxiety and noisy solitude do neither much nor well."

Often busyness is connected to accumulation, and that includes reputation as well as money. Jesus said, "What good will it be for a man if he gains the whole world, yet forfeits his soul?"

Find a life of balance. There's a little word that can help you put a lid on busyness: *No.* Say it to others and to yourself.

"Some go to church and think about fishing,

others go fishing and think about God."

TONY BLAKE

"*The fishing was good; it was the catching that was bad.*"

A.K. BEST

A Slippery Tale

IT'S EMBARRASSING. There's no other word for it. You're just walking along and you trip over your feet or miss a step, and splat! you fall on your face. If any of your friends are around to see it, you know what you're going to hear about the rest of the day!

Years ago I was trout fishing with some friends on the Madison River near Ennis, Montana. It was a beautiful, clear day, and as I walked around the bank I noticed an island with some deep pools alongside it. They just had to be filled with lunkers. So I began wading across the river. The water wasn't overly deep, but the bottom was covered with round slippery rocks. I was careful and made it across. I was right. The fish were there and hungry.

From time to time a raft floated by filled with people either fishing or just enjoying the float trip. After an hour, I was ready to wade back. For some reason the current seemed a bit stronger. I was concerned about slipping on the rocks and was especially cautious when I looked upstream and saw a raft on its way. If I fell, I didn't want it to happen in front of all those people.

That would be humiliating and, worse yet, they were probably armed with video cameras. So I waited, and we casually waved to one another as they glided past. When I didn't think they could see me, I took my first step—on a rock that gave way. I slipped and fell in. My bottom bounced off the river rocks, and since my eyes were open I looked up and could see the surface. I thrust downward with my feet and came upright with my arms in the air clutching my rod. (Actually, that's what I cared about. I didn't want to lose it.) I looked around. No one saw me. Yes! That too was important. I kept wading, got across, and besides being soaked, was none the worse for wear.

As I thought about my mishap, it occurred to me that it was a good metaphor for life. Falling is common in life. We slip on our promises, commitments, and even convictions. When we do fall, the important thing is to get back up and continue the journey, not getting hung up on the embarrassments, the consequences, the pain. Life is filled with opportunities to move forward. I encourage you to keep on keeping on.

The Weigh-In

YOU ENTER AN ARENA in Greensboro, North Carolina. Close to 30,000 people are sitting in the stands waiting for the main event to begin. No, it's not a NASCAR race. It's the Bass Masters Classic weigh-in. Can you imagine that many people sitting there to watch a bunch of fish being weighed? But it's happening more and more. Bass fishing is becoming a major spectator sport on TV and at tournaments. This is one of the few sports where people can get close to their heroes. Anglers come from as far away as Japan to participate.

Anyone can fish tournaments. Competitions are small and local or national. Entry fees vary from a few dollars to thousands. Local clubs hold tournaments and members can team up to compete.

In a major money event, you're matched with another person. Your goal—bring back the largest five bass you can catch. Every ounce counts. You bring all your knowledge, ability, and skill to the forefront in a tournament.

Some pros follow a fishing circuit 30 to 40 percent of the year. They live in motels, drive $70,000 to $100,000 rigs (vehicle and boat) across the country from one lake to another or one river to another. It's quite draining. Pros have to be proficient in many areas—lures (plastics, sizes, and colors); maintenance of boat, trailer, and trucks; lunar tables; weather; and water. In addition, they have to develop strong social skills. If they have sponsors, they're speaking, teaching, and connecting with people in commercial booths at various sporting shows. It's not an easy life.

Some tournaments draw huge crowds. And I'm not talking about 50 people. I mean 5,000 or more. That happened in 1996 at the KILT-FM 100 Bass Tournament in Texas. Anyone could participate for an entry fee of $100. And it didn't matter what you fished out of. You could have a bass boat, rowboat, johnboat, or pontoon. Someone called it the angling equivalent to the Oklahoma land rush. And this tournament pays big time. Every hour an angler is paid $10,000 for the biggest fish. And it's possible to win more than once! If everything works perfectly, you could walk away with $80,000—if you catch the biggest bass in each of the 8 hours. (What are the odds of that?)

"I get all the truth I need in the newspaper every morning, and every chance I get I go fishing, or swap stories with fishermen to get the taste of it out of my mouth."

ED ZERN

You've probably watched the really big tournaments where the top prize is $70,000 and up. Wal-Mart's Forest Wood Open gives the largest purse: $200,000 to the top pro and $49,000 to the top amateur. Bass have really increased in value.[5]

At a Bassmaster tournament in January 2001 at Lake Tohopekaliga and the Kissimmee Chain in Florida, an Arizona pro, Dean Rojas, won $110,000 for first place. What was amazing was his record-breaking total weight for his 4-day limit. Opening day he brought in 45 pounds, 2 ounces, and his total for 4 days was 108 pounds, 12 ounces! Talk about excitement!

Perhaps you've never fished in a bass tournament. Many haven't and never will. But every one of us is in another tournament—the Tournament of Life. And no one has to be a loser. Every one of us can be a winner. We can all come out on top no matter how we've messed up in the past. All that's needed is to take a step of commitment to Jesus. It's a decision worth exploring and experiencing. Check it out!

Lure Wisdom

Bass tend to be visual feeders, and visibility decreases as
the clouds intensify. You can have a great catch on cloudy days
if you use large and/or noisy lures. The darker the cloud cover,
the better to use the noisier and topwater lures. The finish of your
lure is important when the clouds are out. Change from a reflective
finish to a flat (bone white) or hot (orange, chartreuse).
Let them see your lure.

DON WIRTH

"The Weather and Bass" *Bassmaster*, April 2001

"I WAS A HUNTER AND FISHERMAN,
AND MANY A TIME I HAVE SLIPPED OUT INTO
THE WOODS AND PRAIRIES AT 4 A.M. AND
BROUGHT HOME PLENTY OF GAME, OR HAVE
GONE IN A CANOE TO THE COVE AND BROUGHT
BACK A GOOD SUPPLY OF FRESH FISH."

JAY COOKE

Landing a Monster

WHAT'S YOUR BASS fishing dream? If you're like most, it's landing that 10-pounder. Many anglers spend their entire lives chasing that goal. They go from state to state, lake to lake, guide to guide, hoping one day to connect with that wonderful lunker. Some people fish for 30 to 40 years, yet this great fish weight eludes them. I know guides who have yet to connect.

What's a 10-pound bass like? Why is he so difficult to catch? Oops! There's the first misbelief—he. It's not usually the male you want to catch. Fish experts tell us that a male bass rarely gets above 6 pounds. It's the female that does…and she can get big! Some have mouths big enough that you could double both fists and put them inside.

One of the best-known bass pros is Shaw Grigsby. In one year he landed 10 bass over 10 pounds…and all in the same lake. In his book *Bass Master Shaw Grigsby*, he talks about another angler, Doug Hannon, who has caught more than 500 bass over 10 pounds. Can you even imagine such a feat? It was interesting to hear what he said about catching them. He beat the normal conditions. Almost all bass were caught in shallow water and most between ten in the morning and three in the afternoon.[6]

During the first two years of the Lunker Club (catches over 10 pounds) for *Bassmaster* magazine, 278 catches

were submitted. March and April led the months when the most were caught, followed by January and February. Almost 40 percent hit in water between 60 and 70 degrees. Plastic worms, live shiners, jig-and-pig, and spinnerbaits were the top four lures or baits. Florida (26.6 percent), Texas (18.7 percent), and California (16.2 percent) led the states in catches. Lake Fork in Texas led the list of the most lunker catches during this time (32).

What's your largest bass so far? What's your dream? Like most, I wanted to catch that huge monster. But not really getting into bass fishing until I was in my late fifties, I wondered about the possibilities. In the spring of 2000 I went on a couple of outings with well-known California guide Bob Crupi. On my first trip with him to Castaic Lake I hit a 9-pound, 2-ounce beauty. I was delighted. That was my biggest fish up to that point. But the next month I landed a 10-pound, 1-ounce bass. It was hard to believe. During her first rush we didn't think she was that large. But then she came out from under a buoy line, went under the boat, and tried to circle the anchor rope. All I could think was keep the pressure on, reel when she stops, and don't let the 8-pound line hit the bottom of the boat. And when we scooped her into the net it was a huge thrill. (That was the same day I caught a 7-pounder and two 5-pounders!)

How did I happen to snag these monsters? It wasn't due to my knowledge and skill, that's for sure. I listened to Bob and followed his directions to the letter. And it took patience. A lot of patience.

It's easy to miss out on opportunities because we don't follow the life principle of patience. Impatient decisions and acts not only cause people to miss out on what they want, but it can lead to results they regret the rest of their lives.

Even a little thing such as impatience in what you say has far-reaching results. A biblical proverb says, "Do you see a man who speaks in haste? There is more hope for a fool than for him." What's your degree of patience in what you say?

And how are you about being taught? Are you a good student? How would your family members describe your openness to instruction?

Shaw Grigsby has some final instructions on catching 10-pounders: To catch them, you have to do everything right. And even if you do, it could be years before you hook one…if you hook one.[9]

"Caution is the most valuable asset in fishing, especially if you are the fish."

AUTHOR UNKNOWN

Age: A Fact of Life

IF YOU CAUGHT a 2-pound bass in Oklahoma, how old do you think it was? And what if you caught a 2-pound bass in the Mississippi River between Iowa and Illinois. How old was *that* one? You'd probably say, "Come on, they're both the same." Not necessarily. The Mississippi is a muddy river, and a bass living there can take 5 years to reach 12 inches. The Okie fish, on the other hand, grows much faster. It has clearer water and a longer growing season. There's a lot of variation since there are many factors involved.

But who wants to know about a 2-pounder? We all want trophy bass. How old are they? Do you recall how to tell the age of a pine tree? You count the annual rings. According to fish biologists, you can accurately figure out a bass's age by counting the growth rings from almost any bony structure of its body. When a fish grows, a new bony structure is added in circular fashion, just like the rings of growth you see on trees. And unlike many mammals that reach their full size in two or three years, bass keep growing.

Where's the best place to look? At their scales. By measuring the distance between these rings and knowing the length of the fish, a fish biologist can calculate the length of any fish at a given age.[8]

It's one thing to note the length and weight of that trophy bass, but the next time you catch one, see if you can determine its age. The bass won't mind. He's not sensitive about it like we are. We seem to have this hang-up about getting older and letting others know our "real" age. Aging is just part of life. How old are you? No, we're not going to count the rings on your skin or gray hairs on your head.

In the Bible, getting older and being older is counted as a blessing. It's a time of honor. Sure, there are lots of changes we don't particularly care for. The biblical King Solomon described these:

> *"These brook trout*
> *will strike any fly you present,*
> *provided you don't get*
> *close enough to present it."*
>
> DICK BLALOCK

THE KEEPERS OF THE HOUSE TREMBLE, AND THE STRONG MEN STOOP, WHEN THE GRINDERS CEASE BECAUSE THEY ARE FEW, AND THOSE LOOKING THROUGH THE WINDOWS GROW DIM; WHEN THE DOORS TO THE STREET ARE CLOSED AND THE SOUND OF GRINDING FADES; WHEN MEN RISE UP AT THE SOUND OF BIRDS, BUT ALL THEIR SONGS GROW FAINT; WHEN MEN ARE AFRAID OF HEIGHTS AND OF DANGERS IN THE STREETS; WHEN THE ALMOND TREE BLOSSOMS AND THE GRASSHOPPER DRAGS HIMSELF ALONG AND DESIRE NO LONGER IS STIRRED.

That's fairly blunt. Aging is a fact of life. We think a lot about it. Bass don't. Perhaps they're the fortunate ones. We need to number our days in this brief life to make sure none end up missing, that we don't squander a day, since every one is a gift.

With nary one fish to show for his day with rod and reel, an amateur fisherman stopped at a market on his way home and thoughtfully bought a dozen trout. He then ordered the fish man to throw them to him one at a time.

"When I tell my wife," he explained to the mystified fish man, "that I catch fish—I catch them!"

BENNETT CERF

Is It Always This Easy?

FORK LAKE. Most of us who have been bass fishing for any length of time have heard stories about this lake. It's got a fantastic reputation. And it deserves it. The number of bass over 10 pounds caught there is astounding.

A guide shared an experience with me that he could have done without though. It seems that a man met a woman in a hotel bar in San Diego. The program on the bar's TV described the fishing at Fork Lake in Texas. All it took was one comment from the woman— "I'd sure love to go fishing there"—and the man said, "Let's do it." They weren't even sure where Fork Lake was, but they figured if they could fly into Dallas, they'd locate it. They asked around, rented a car, arrived at the lake, and found a guide. They made arrangements for fishing the next morning. Before they parted, the guide told them to bring some warm clothes. He was surprised when he heard back, "Hey, this is all we have…just what you see on us." So the guide said he'd bring some extra stuff with him. He brought a coat for the man and a sleeping bag for the lady friend. She didn't look like she would take to the rigors of the weather or fishing.

The story centers around the guy. When the couple and guide hit the first cove, the guide gave the man a rod and instructed him on what to do: "When the fish hits, set the hook as hard as you can." He knew it was going to be a long day when he heard in reply, "What's that mean, set the hook?" I can just imagine the look on the guide's face, the thoughts that went through his mind, and what he was tempted to say. He kept his cool, gave some more instruction, and went to fishing. An hour later the San Diego man had boated a 10-pounder. An hour later an 11-pounder came aboard, which led the guy to ask a profound question: "Hey, is catching these big bass always this easy?" Now, there's a death-wish question. I know guides who have fished 20 years and are still working on their first double-digit bass.

The couple probably went back to San Diego and spread a distorted view of bass fishing all around town. Of course, most fishing experiences after one like that are downhill.

This guy is like many others who believe everything in life ought to come easy. They don't spend time learning, practicing, improving their skill, or working hard. Their motto is, "If it don't come easy, it ain't worth it."

Since more men than women are probably reading this book, let's focus on men. Some guys are selectively lazy. They're workhorses at the office, and that's good. But what do their garages look like? What about workrooms, backyards, or catchall drawers? How are you doing in this department? If you're married, how would your wife rate you on productivity around the homestead? Yeah, you're right. Bad question! But it's necessary to ask. Why? Simply because a number of men have MPP—Multiple Personality Problem. They're supercharged workers on the job, but at home they function like lazy hound dogs. And to make matters worse (much worse!), if their wives know they're giving their all at the office, they will not be happy receiving only leftovers at home.

So what's the answer? Consistent productivity—at work and at home. God calls us to do our best and to give our best—everywhere. Is it easy? No. Attainable? Definitely.

"My wife wonders why all women do not seek anglers for husbands. She has come in contact with many in her life with me and she claims that they all have a sweetness in their nature which others lack."

RAY BERGMAN

Who Is Really in Control?

MOST ANGLERS WANT to be in control. You can see it in the way they walk to the dock or launch their boat. It's evident in what they say and how they say it. What they really want is to be in control of their fishing. To some degree we *can* be in charge. We can buy the best equipment, keep it in the best repair, sharpen our hooks, retie our knots periodically, and study bass. This much we can control.

But once our bait hits the water, we have little control as to when the fish hits, how hard, and where. The big issue is who's in control once that bass hits. We want to control him, and he wants to get away from us. So what we have is one big power struggle. Some anglers land almost all the fish they hook. They're in charge. Others lose more than they land because they let the bass take over.

What's the best way to control a bass? Shaw Grigsby suggests the following:

- Try to keep him from changing directions.
- If he runs through heavy cover, let him run.
- Keep him in view so you can react.
- Don't do anything else when you're fighting a fish.
- Keep him down in the water.
- Don't relax when he gets close to the boat. Expect him to try to jump at the boat.[9]

Following these simple suggestions can give us more control, but we must realize there are many aspects of fishing—as well as of life—we'll never be able to control, no matter how hard we try.

Some people never seem to get the message that they can't control everything. They keep trying and trying. They push, pull, persuade, manipulate, and withdraw. Yes, withdraw. Silence and withdrawal are great ways to control others. Sometimes these folks even try to control cats. Have you ever tried to control a cat? It's a losing battle. There's no way to accomplish that feat. Cats are incorrigible character disorders.

What prompts this lifestyle of trying to control?

Control is a camouflage for fear. Who wants to be afraid or even admit they are? Not me. Not you. Fear makes us feel vulnerable. If others knew we were afraid,

they'd take advantage of us. So we hide our fear by going on the offense. But the Bible says, "There is no fear in love...Perfect love drives out fear."

Control is a cover-up for insecurity. A secure person doesn't need to always be in control. He can defer to others, ask their advice, be comfortable when someone else leads. To feel safe we sometimes go overboard by trying to control everything and everyone. There's an emptiness within us when we're insecure; we're like a bucket with a hole in it. We can never get filled up, but we keep trying to add water.

Control is a cover-up for low self-esteem. When we feel down on ourselves, worthless, or lacking, we don't want others to know about it. We may even blame them for helping to create the problem. What better way to overcome this than by making others pay through our control? But we're fooling ourselves. Control never fulfills because it never solves the basic problem. It simply perpetuates it. It never draws others closer but rather pushes them away. And we end up feeling worse.

So what's the answer? Give up control. Hand the reins of your life to God. When He is in charge, you'll be amazed at how much better your relationships with others will be.

Ol' Bucket Mouth

'VE HEARD HIM referred to as garbage disposal or terminator, but his usual name is Ol' Bucket Mouth. His mouth isn't just big, it's huge. Did you know a bass will grab and digest any food that fits into its mouth? Lizards, snakes, turtles, and dragonflies go down the hatch. But that's not all! Let a mouse or even a rat fall into the water, and it could end up being digested. That's why when you look through the Bass Pro catalog you'll see rat and mouse lures. And how about a nice fluffy duckling or a big fat frog? Bass love both.

One day I was fishing from shore, casting a rubber frog onto a patch of green scum and slowly twitching my offering back. Right below where I was standing the scum stopped and the water was clear. I was hunkered down, about three feet from the surface. I flicked my frog into the clear water. All of a sudden I saw this steel trap of a mouth ascending from under the water. The movie Jaws flashed through my mind. The bass came straight out of the water, missing the frog. I swear—if it had tonsils I could have counted them. I was so shocked I jumped up and backward, yelled, and startled a jogger on the adjacent path. (The reason the bass missed the frog was because I jerked it away when he spooked me.) That mouth was huge!

When a bass attacks a school of minnows, he's like a mowing machine in a field of wheat. He likes to swallow his food whole, and he's got an expandable belly (not unlike some others I know). But he's also adept at picking up food off the river bottom, using his mouth like tweezers. I've seen bass with red, bruised lips from hitting the rocks as they go after crawdads.

With that mouth, if a bass could talk, he'd probably talk your arm and leg off (if he didn't bite them off first). He's the fish that would be saying, "Oops, why'd I say that? I stuck my fin in my mouth again." His mouth could get him into trouble. So can ours. Some anglers resemble bass in more ways than one, and it's not always pleasant.

How can you handle "Largemouth Syndrome"? Don't boast. Keep to the truth and don't exaggerate. Don't flatter. We know how to butter-up someone, especially when we want something…like learning the favorite spots of top anglers! Guard against this. Don't run off at the mouth. Keep the air around you free from empty words that clutter the atmosphere with useless information. Avoid arguments. Strife implies rigidity, stubbornness, and unhealthy anger. Do speak softly and with authority. Gentleness usually accomplishes more than force.

The book of Proverbs contains more than 150 references to tongue, mouth, lips, and words. If you want more insights, check out this unique book of wisdom!

"The true fisherman approaches the first day of fishing season with all the sense of wonder and awe of a child approaching Christmas."

ROBERT TRAVER

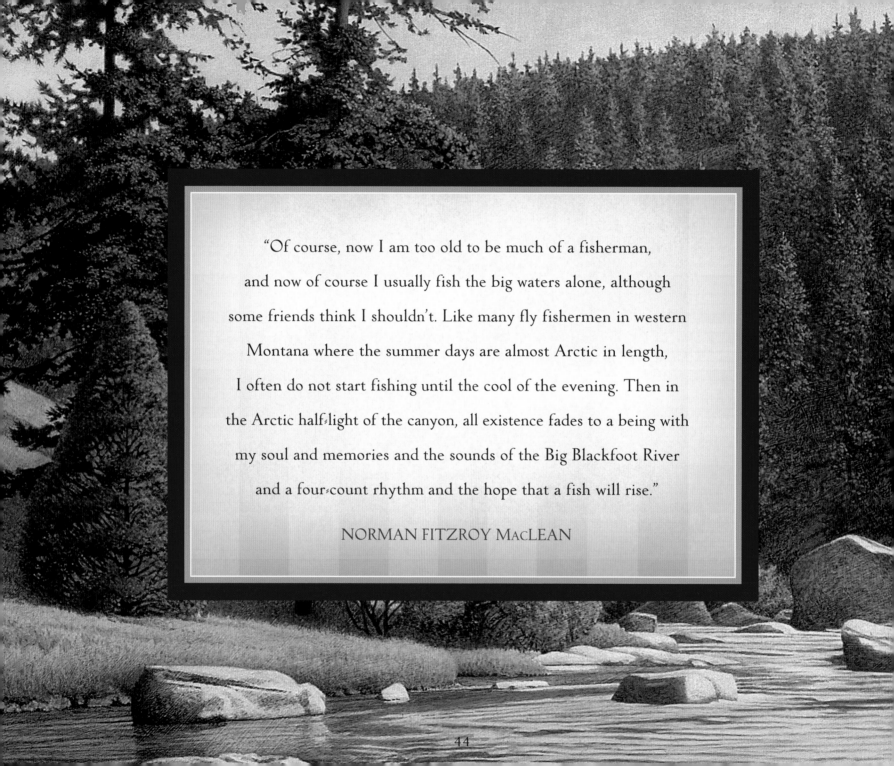

"Of course, now I am too old to be much of a fisherman,

and now of course I usually fish the big waters alone, although

some friends think I shouldn't. Like many fly fishermen in western

Montana where the summer days are almost Arctic in length,

I often do not start fishing until the cool of the evening. Then in

the Arctic half-light of the canyon, all existence fades to a being with

my soul and memories and the sounds of the Big Blackfoot River

and a four-count rhythm and the hope that a fish will rise."

NORMAN FITZROY MacLEAN

"All Americans believe that they are born fishermen. For a man to admit to a distaste for fishing would be like denouncing mother-love and hating moonlight."

JOHN STEINBECK

The Tribute

I WENT SHORE FISHING the other day and took a friend with me. In fact, I went more for him than for myself. He hadn't been fishing in a while. You see, he's getting old. It's harder for him to get around, and his hearing is going as well. He was quite excited when I told him we were going to the lake. The shore was easier for him than sitting in the old junk boat I keep at this reservoir.

We walked out on an old weed-filled road to the dam, since bass had been schooling there recently. I was bent on getting out there to fish, but my friend seemed to notice the foliage and wildlife around us. I took a cue from him, slowed down, and saw what I'd been missing.

As we sat on the dam I began casting out over the sloping bottom. I alternated between a purple worm and a green-fleck Yamamoto spider jig. My friend just sat on a towel, content to watch me catch and release a dozen bass and rattle on about nothing significant. I probably repeated stories he'd heard before, but it didn't bother him like it does some people. Now and then he'd get up and come over to take a closer look at a bass I'd caught. Of course, he's seen many fish in his time. He's even had fish slap him in the head as they were lifted into the boat.

As we walked the half-mile back to the car, I noticed how his pace had slowed. He seemed weary, and it was an effort to get into the van. I told him just to rest

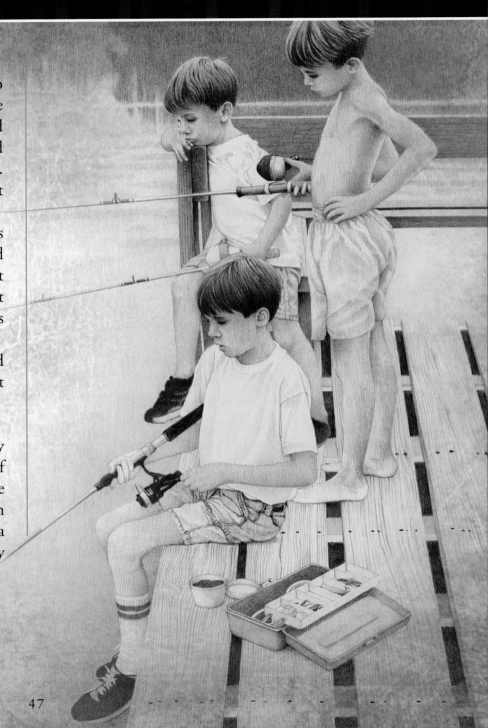

while we drove back to the house. We didn't need to talk. I wondered how many more times he'd be able to go fishing with me. I guess we just take it for granted that we'll always be able to fish. Have you ever wondered about that? Most of us just assume nothing will change. I know that one day he won't be able to go. I don't look forward to that day at all.

He's an excellent sight fisherman. He'll spot a bass that I've missed on the shoreline or next to a rock. And he'll stay with that fish until it's caught. What's great about him is the fact that he usually gives me the first opportunity to catch it. Once in a great while he gets a bit impatient and goes for it himself.

He's got an uncanny ability to spot crawdads and other critters under the water too. I've learned a lot from him, and there's still more to learn from him.

My friend has been special in other ways as well.

He came into my life about six months after my son died. For both my wife and me he was a source of comfort during our journey through grief. But we aren't the only ones he's helped. A few years later when my mom was spending her last two months in a convalescent home, I'd visit each day and take my friend with me.

Fishing does not build character. It reveals it.
WYSE ORTHA

He connected so well with the other residents that some of them would sit in the lobby for hours waiting to see him. And when they did, their faces, which most of the time had no expression, brightened, and a rare smile emerged. Several would congregate around him, and his gentle touch and silent presence brought delight, comfort, and a bright spot into a day of drab routine. He'd smile at each one and either put his head or a paw in their lap.

Sometimes I'd share stories with them about how Sheffield would stalk turtles or crawdads in my small backyard pond. One day he was putting his head under the water up to his ears so I put a snorkel on him and took a series of pictures. They laughed when they thought of a 75-pound golden retriever with a snorkel.

A dog for a friend? You bet! He's more faithful, loyal, patient, and fun-loving than a lot of people I know—as well as never tiring of fishing with me.

My friend is no longer with me. Old age caught up with him. I go on without him, but that's all right. No one can take away the rich memories or experiences we've had together, and for those I am grateful. In fact, for every experience I've had fishing, I'm thankful.

God's Word tells us, "In everything give thanks." I'm thankful for living in a country with the freedoms we have. I'm thankful for all the opportunities I've had to fish. I'm thankful for the people and animals who have enriched my life. Most of all, I'm thankful that I know I will spend my future with Jesus, both here on earth and when I've left it. I hope you too have that assurance.

"YOU CAN'T HIT A HOME RUN UNLESS YOU STEP UP TO THE PLATE.
YOU CAN'T CATCH FISH UNLESS YOU PUT YOUR LINE IN THE WATER.
YOU CAN'T REACH YOUR GOALS IF YOU DON'T TRY."

AUTHOR UNKNOWN

*If a man is truly blessed, he returns home from fishing
to be greeted by the best catch of his life.*

AUTHOR UNKNOWN

NOTES

1. Thomas H. Maught, "Study Advice to Husbands: Accept Wife's Influence,"
   Los Angeles Times, Feb. 22, 1998, Section A, 1.

2. Max Lucado, *On the Anvil* (Wheaton, IL: Tyndale House Publishers, 1985),
   69-70.

3. Patrick Morley, *Man in the Mirror* (Brentwood, TN: Wolgemuth and
   Hyatt, 1989), 274-75.

4. Dr. Hal Schramm, "What Does Your Bass Really Weigh?"
   North American Fisherman, Mar. 2001, 37-42, adapted.

5. Richard Louv, *Fly-Fishing for Sharks* (New York: Simon & Schuster, 2000),
   55-56, adapted.

6. Shaw Grigsby, *Bass Master Shaw Grigsby* (Washington, D.C.:
   National Geographic Book, 1998), 131-32, adapted.

7. Ibid., 133, adapted.

8. W. Horace Carter, *How Old Is a Trophy Bass?* (New York: Simon & Schuster,
   2000), 56-57, adapted.

9. Grigsby, *Bass Master Shaw Grigsby,* 112-13, adapted.